THE PERFECT SEX GUIDE

ESSENTIALS YOU MUST KNOW TO TAKE YOUR SEX TO THE NEXT LEVEL

ADAHI FLORES

CONTENTS

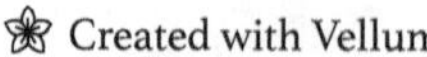 Created with Vellum

INTRODUCTION

I want to thank you and congratulate you for downloading the book "The Perfect Sex Guide."

This book contains proven steps and strategies for overcoming any love problems that you have had and taking your love life to the next level; by using the amazing hot tips in this book, you will experience a more fulfilling love life full of more pleasure with your partner. It also contains advice on how you can continue on the road of progress to make your love and sex life even hotter than before during days when the flame is about to go out.

I know what it's like to suffer from not knowing what to do, how to make your love and sex life spicier, and the stress it can cause in your life. Unfortunately, any drawback is difficult to change, as you get so conditioned to living a certain way.

When you begin to apply the empowering ideas and concepts contained in this book you will no longer be enslaved to your old pattern.

Most advice on taking your love life to a whole new other level is only good for a given number of time. They do not extend to one´s whole life and what a girl might experience through it all. It takes time and the right mindset to blow your partner's mind. In this book, you'll find all of that and more.

By applying the steps in this book, I can guarantee you that you will experience higher levels of pleasure and happiness in your love and sex life and change your life forever. It's not only worked for me but many others that have been through this program.

Thanks again for downloading this book; I hope you enjoy it!

HOW TO HAVE SEX AND THE TRUTH
ABOUT IT

Sex. Depending on where we're like, we may all have a different way of reacting. All women are different people, which means we all have different views about something as natural as sex. You could be the shy type and prefer discussing it in the bedroom and not in public. Or you could be the outspoken type and think it is nothing to be ashamed of because it empowers women as much as it empowers men. But, no matter who we are and how different our lives are, we can't deny one thing—we all think about it. Some may think about it all the time, and others may try their best to refrain from thinking about it when they do. But the point remains, sex is on our minds.

For something so fundamental as sex, it's surprising how shrouded in mystery some of it is. Sometimes, we can't help but wonder whether everything we know about it is true. Where did we hear all of this information anyway? In the movies, on television, on the internet, in the media, or through chitter-chatter of friends? It's not like we get a handbook the minute we enter puberty and a personal tutor to guide us and tell us everything we need to know about it. Sure, we get sex education. But we all know hair growth and menstrual cycles are not what we're wondering about. There comes the point in our lives when we want to really learn the truth about sex. The real, uncensored version of sex. And when it comes to the real details about sex, our parents leave us be. Our teachers leave us be. So we have to find out for ourselves. And that is where this book comes in handy. It's here to finally tell you some truths and tips I think every woman should know about sex, things that you have probably been waiting a very long time to hear.

RELAX, He's Not Scanning You for Flaws

Sex is all about feeling relaxed and comfortable. And this is one of the most important things to remember when you're having sex, especially if it's for the first time or with a certain person for the first time. You might wonder why you didn't have as good a time as you wanted, and the reason could be because you were too worried about how you looked that you weren't able to completely surrender to all the sensations happening to your body. When he sees you naked for the first time, and you're tangled up in each other, he isn't going to waste his time looking at your flabs or your cellulite or your pimple on your forehead. Goodness, no. For men having sex, is the last thing on their minds. So it should be the last thing on yours too. He's not thinking about your flaws, he's thinking about you around him and the pleasure building up inside. So if you want to enjoy the sex as much as he is, you better let go and think about that as well.

KEEP Looking for That Sweet Spot

One thing that is quite reassuring to hear is that so many women have trouble reaching orgasm—if you're experiencing this trouble, you are not alone. It's hard not to worry when you hear stories from your friends left and right about how they are having great sex while you can go a whole relationship with someone and just keep faking it all the way. You might have thought that something was wrong with you and that you should give up on sex altogether, just because what you hear and see on television or even internet porn depicts a completely false picture of women's orgasms. But now I'm telling you that you don't need to lose hope! It exists. Doctors thought most women couldn't climax not too long ago, but now they say that it exists in every woman. Chances are you just haven't found it or the right partner to bring it out. So many women tell stories about how they thought it was hopeless, and then one day, they just found it. The search is worth it.

THE MORE YOU Worry About Your Orgasm, The More It Won't Come.

Great sex is all about being relaxed. If you've got a lot on your mind at the time, even if your worries are concerning sex, it won't help your body ease into the pleasure of lovemaking. To have great sex, you need to surrender to every feeling and let it take you, body and mind. You need to get vulnerable and feel him taking charge inside you. You need to feel the sensations, and you should definitely not stress over them, or else your body might just think to take the hint that it is a stressful process and it might withhold the orgasm all the more.

DON'T BE Stingy on Masturbation

Some people think that the only time a girl needs to pleasure herself is when she's going through a dry spell. Granted, it does take the edge off of things if you haven't gotten laid in a while. But masturbation doesn't have to be something you only resort to when you're not getting great sex. It can even make your sex better. When you masturbate, your body often gets primed sexually more often than it normally does, which makes you more open to sex and even makes your body look for it. Think of it as a pep talk or practice before the big game. By the time your guy comes around, you'll feel nice and ready. Knowing how to touch yourself also makes it easier for you to get an orgasm. You can bring this about by yourself, but you can also teach him how you like to be touched to help him make you come when you're with your partner.

You Don't Need To Be A Magician To Make Him Climax

Men are pretty simple creatures, and the same is true in the bedroom. When you're having sex, don't worry about being inexperienced or knowing what makes him tick. That's their thing to worry about. Just because we as women are incredibly complicated creatures in the bedroom, it doesn't mean we should think men are puzzles as well. This is where we're lucky because even just the basics are enough to get a man to come. Don't get insecure about sex because you don't know any fancy tricks, be confident and know that he is getting just as much pleasure as you are.

Warm Yourself Up

If you're a busy person that has a lot of things on her to-do list, chances are it will take you a while before you're ready to pounce. Real-life isn't like porn where you're swamped with work, and a hot guy comes in, and you drop everything and are revved up to go. Chances are when you get home, you are tired and sleepy, and having sex isn't going to be as enjoyable as you would want it to be. To get yourself in the mood and to rebalance yourself, you could take some alone time first. Get into the shower and breathe, or spend a couple of minutes unwind. That way, when your partner puts his arms around you, it will be perfect timing, and you'll be ready to make love. Even foreplay can be used to get you in the mood, and in the next chapter, we'll find out how.

FOREPLAY

*I*f you want to be guided on how to have great sex, then take note of this step. Now, everyone knows you need to warm up before you do any strenuous physical activity if you want it to go well. But don't worry, I wasn't talking about doing jumping jacks or stretching before you, and your man gets hot and steamy. What I mean by warming up is getting yourself ready to make love. Foreplay is an essential part of any woman's sex life because it gets her in the mood. Men may say that they can skip foreplay altogether, but women can't. We need it. This is because we are more complicated, and it takes a lot more to start our engine if you want to make sure that it keeps running until the end. So if you or your man want to have great sex, you need to know what to do to get yourself warmed up the best.

DIRTY TALK

This is one great way to get a woman's blood burning—in a good way. Women love communication, we always want more of it, and it's no surprise that it's the same case in the bedroom. Now, sometimes your man might not be the first one who would try it. But normally, when you start talking dirty to him, he'll start talking dirty back as well. Also, if you talk dirty to him, it can turn you on just as much as it can turn him on. Sometimes, all they need is a little push. It's great fun when you try it way before you're in the bedroom. Try this: while you're having dinner out, you could whisper in his ear that you're wet for him. That alone could get his blood boiling, and he could respond in turn and say that he's hard. Then, you can talk about how you both masturbate. Since you both will have to hold it in, the sexual tension will be built up so much that it will just explode in the bedroom by the time you get home. You can also talk dirty to him in the bedroom by just describing what you're feeling during sex in a soft, slow voice while keeping eye contact. Moaning and sighing also get both of you turned on.

Kissing All Over

A passionate kiss on the lips is always a good turn-on, but to get you really turned on for sex, your man needs to explore other areas. If he seems to be spending too much time on your lips and then going straight to the grand finale, you can always tell him that you would like attention in other areas. If you don't want to voice it out, you can always direct him gently with your hands. A great way for you to feel stimulated is if he starts kissing your neck. The breath and heat on this sensitive part of your skin are enough to make you feel very hot, not to mention the feeling of his head caressing that area. He can also whisper dirty things in your ear and then start kissing it, his breath tickling you and making you want more. Of course, there's also the breasts, which he can kiss or suck however way he wants. I'm sure he'll like spending time there too; you can even make him play with them.

. . .

Play With the Twins

As I said above, the breasts are an important part you don't want to miss if you want to get yourself aroused. Making him kiss you while letting him squeeze your breasts can get you turned on even more. But you can also play around yourself. You can stroke them and squeeze your nipples, making sounds in the process. By making him watch you touch yourself, not only will he get insanely aroused, but you'll also feel incredibly sexy and more confident in yourself. This will allow you to feel more relaxed when it's time to do it.

Being Touched Down There

This is a great way to get aroused, and the best thing about it is that if you masturbate, you can teach him all the ropes. Slowly guide his hand down there when you're ready, and he'll pretty much take the hint. You can even spice it up and start this going in the car so that the sexual tension builds. Then, when he's down there, tell him exactly how you like it, and you can even let him watch you do it so he'll learn.

Oral Sex

This gets women so turned on that sometimes we can even climax at this point, before any of the penetration happens. If you want your guy to concentrate a little down there, you can gently guide his head and give him hints. Most women like it when he starts it slow and slowly builds, by kissing and licking around before he stimulates the clitoris. How he does, it depends entirely on you and what gets you turned on, but the most important thing is that you guide him through it like anything else.

Now that we've gotten through everything leading up to this point, it's time for the grand finale. When you both are sufficiently aroused and are ready, it's time for you to decide what positions you will take. Keep in mind; I said positions. You don't have to stick to just one for the whole night; variety is the spice in life. So if you feel like your normal fallback position isn't quite doing the job, you should try out others— your partner will feel excited about experimenting too. This chapter talks about the positions known to make women orgasm the most.

Modified Missionary

The simplest positions with a few tweaks are the key to achieving female orgasm. The idea behind this is that when you're not distracted by keeping your balance or bending your body in a weird way, you can fully concentrate on all the sensations and surrender yourself to the pleasure.

· · ·

THIS POSITION IS like the missionary, except both your legs are over his shoulders, as if your body is folded in half. You should also put a pillow underneath your butt so that your hips are higher than the rest of your body. This aligns both of you together, and it allows him to thrust in deeper and have greater penetration. A great thing about this position is that it hits you in just the right spot—your G-spot. This is a sensitive area inside your vagina that feels like a raspberry to touch and is a very tough spot to reach. This position rubs it in just the right way and gets you warmed up much faster. Now, once you feel like your G-spot is ready, put your legs down and make him align his pelvic bone with your clitoris and stroke it with his body during his thrusts. The warming up of your G-spot and the stimulation of your clitoris will then bring you to climax.

Cowgirl

Now, this is a really reliable position to bring yourself to orgasm, and the magic behind it is because you have control. He is on the floor facing up in this position, and you are sitting on him, with your legs spread wide and you facing him. You can steady yourself with your hands and then slowly thrust up and down. Not only can you stimulate your clitoris, but this position also frees up his hands so he can do it as well. You can even make him sit up so that you can kiss him and caress him, and you can also rub your clitoris against his body until you both reach climax.

Reverse Cowgirl

This position is the same as the one above, except now you are facing his feet. This time, keep your legs together instead of spreading wide and slowly thrust up and down. With your legs closed, your G-spot is stimulated much more this way, making it a lot tighter. It has the same benefits as the position above, and you can concentrate on exactly how you want the thrusts to go and how deep since, for once, you are dictating the movement.

Modified Doggy Style

Some women may not like this position just because of its name; it can also feel awkward. But when you modify it, it doesn't look as weird, and it can also make you reach climax even more. This position is the doggy style, except you are lying down with your butt lifted to position yourself to enter you. With your clitoris against the bed, you can rub it up and down together with his thrusts until you climax. You can also lift your butt and adjust his entry angle so that he's hitting just the right spot you want. It's also easier to keep the angle in this position than when you're lying down on your back. But as much as this position is a good modification, some people also prefer the good old doggy-style. It's no problem because experts also say that the original doggy style can also help you orgasm, and some people find it fun and dirty.

Pinball Wizard

This position gets it's name for the way your man holds you like a pinball machine. You need to be lying on your back and your man needs to be in front of you kneeling down on the bed. Now slowly lift up your hips until your butt is off the ground, and let him hold you that way by grasping under your thighs. Then he can start thrusting himself in while you help him by raising your torso a little bit, with your arms and elbows supporting your weight. Imagine a diagonal line from his head to your head, and try to make your body parallel to that line as much as possible. This position is not only fun, it's easy for him also to massage your mons pubis. If you want deeper penetration you can swing your leg over his shoulder.

Magic Mountain

If you want all the benefits of penetration and clitoral stimulation and want to be comfortable and intimate with your partner, you should try this position. It is called Magic Mountain because of the mountain shapes your bent knees make. First, you both need to be facing each other with your legs bent, so they look like two little mountains. Next, you can lean back on your hands if you feel off-balanced. Then, you can ease into him slowly while you both are in this position, and you can be face to face with each other the whole time. This position is great because you both have equal control, and you can both control the thrusting and his motions. You can even stimulate your clitoris with your free hand, and he can sit back and just watch you go. Some people recommend sliding an ice cube down his chest and feeling the icy water pool in the pelvic area where you both are connected. It's great because this position isn't like the others that require fancy aerobics, and no one has to be lifting anything or struggling, so you can really concentrate on getting your orgasm.

Get On The Table

Not only does this make you a little bit more excited about adding another element to having sex, but it also helps you reach climax. What you need to do is get up on a table or even the kitchen counter, lie down, and put your butt close to the edge. Now he should be standing in front of you in between your legs and thrusting in and out while your legs are on his shoulders. Since you both are in completely relaxed positions, he can stroke your body all over or even stimulate your clit. If you want to help, try to lift your butt while clenching it, this lets blood flow into the area and gives you a better chance of orgasming.

Spooning

Of course, there is this intimate position. For this position, you're both on your sides lying down on the bed, and he is inside you. Since we know that women are complicated creatures, and they also need to feel intimacy and love to be able to climax, this snuggly position scores high on both emotional and physical aspects. He should keep it inside you and just keep thrusting against your vagina's front wall, where your G-spot is. While you're in this position, he can play with your clitoris and even breathe into your ear and the back of your neck. This will surely lead you to orgasm.

TIPS ABOUT SEX

*D*oesn't it feel great now that you know all about sex in the real, truthful, uncensored way? However, now that you think that you're prepared to have great orgasmic sex, there are a few more things that you need to keep in mind that relate to sex as well. Even if you have great sex now and have successfully reached climax multiple times, there could still be some thoughts that cross your mind and worry you about sex. I hope these tips will help you with them, and I would just like to give you some last-minute advice for the road. So as a parting gift, here are some facts and tips about sex for your sexy times ahead!

It's Not Just Men—Women Think About Sex Too. A Lot!

Everyone says that sex is always on a man's mind, and they shake their heads as if this is totally wrong. But women think about sex a lot as well. In fact, when you think about it, there's really no reason we shouldn't. It's funny how as little girls and throughout our lives growing up, and we are taught by the world everything about us as women. Our rights and what we should uphold in ourselves. Our emotions and how we should take care and love ourselves while finding our place in this world. We are even taught about our bodies and how we should and should not use them. Imagine, our parents or our schools have given us almost a 360-degree view of ourselves as women, except there is one vital factor lacking. Sex. So it's only natural that sex is on our minds. Women think about sex as much as some men do, and the sooner we accept that this is normal, the sooner we can be comfortable enough to learn more about the different ways you can make your sex life better.

You Can Never Have "Too Much" Sex

Women are so used to being viewed negatively when people find out they are having "too much" sex. But the truth is, there is no such thing as a "sex quota" you have to follow. What destroys great sex is worrying about it too much. It just ruins the moment when you're forcing it even if you don't want it because you feel you're having too little sex or when you hold back because you think it's becoming too much. Every person is different, and every couple is even more different, so you don't need to add any more unnecessary tension to your sex life by feeling pressured about the number of times you do it.

Your Sweet Spot Is Not Going to Stay in The Same Spot

If the time comes that you notice your magical spot is not giving you the same pleasure anymore, it isn't something to worry about. Women's needs change all the time, and the way you made love in your 20's will probably not be the same way you'd want in your 30's. A woman likes to try new things, and your body knows that even if your head doesn't. If your sweet spot changes, you just need to look for where your new one is and what turns you on now.

There's No Expiration Date for Sex, It Only Gets Better As You Age

You don't peak when you're in your twenties, unlike what a lot of people believe. Many people might worry about when they will be able to get an orgasm because they think they're operating on some kind of insane time limit. But the thing is, sex isn't just good when you're young. It actually gets better as you both grow older. This is because, as in any skill, practice makes perfect. As you grow older, not only do you know your partner more and vice versa, you also know yourself more. It'll be easier for you to understand what gets you going, and you have your whole life to take your time and figure it our. Women also experience multiple orgasms more in the later stages of their life, like the 40s, 50s, or 60s compared to when they were in their 20s.

The End.

Did You Like This Book? Then You Will LOVE How to Love Yourself and Fall in Love.

"How to Love Yourself and Fall in Love Now contains proven steps and strategies on how to learn how to open yourself up to love and learn that to truly fall in love, you have to learn to love yourself as well.

If there is one thing all of mankind would probably agree on, there is nothing in this world that is quite like love. If the people of the world can argue and disagree about views, laws, religion, and anything at all, this is one truth that we all believe. Love is the thread that runs through each of our lives and binds us all together. Love gives us a reason to fight and a reason to heal. Love gives us a reason to live and a reason to die for. No matter how much people in this world would like the rest to believe that something as tender and as vulnerable as love is at the center of all of our lives, we cannot deny the truth. Love is what makes us human.

Start Reading How to Love Yourself and Fall in Love NOW!

HTTPS://BOOKS2READ.COM/U/38YQP6

SNEAK PEEK - CHAPTER 1

Start Reading How to Love Yourself and Fall in Love NOW!

https://books2read.com/u/38yQP6

The Beauty of Love

ONE THING I love about humans is that no matter how much we deny it, our whole world revolves around love. It's in everything we find beautiful, it's in everything we hold dear. It's in every place the sunshine touches, it's in fingertips and flower petals and the warmth of another heart against yours. But the concept of love even exists in places where the sun doesn't shine, among the most hardened of souls, between the lines of the darkest of issues. All these things are the way they are because they are somehow connected to love. The lack of love. The misuse of love. The battle for love. Wars have been waged in the name of love—protecting your family, your loved ones. Evil acts have been done out of love, crazed, dangerous love. Yet, even the darkest of souls have probably loved something, or someone, once in their life. When you open your eyes long enough to look, you'll see that it is simply everywhere.

I AM willing to say almost every action a human being makes can somehow be traced back to love.

AND ONE THING I love about *love* is that it is, in truth, such a useless emotion when you think about it. It is not useless in the sense that it should be done away with, but vain in that it doesn't serve a real purpose. Among all our mighty survival instincts and feelings, love seems much too tender to help us survive. Take a look at anger, it is needed to fight for what you think is your body's best interests.

TAKE A LOOK AT BRAVERY, it is required to protect what is important to you. Even sadness trains you to avoid losing what means most to you the way happiness rewards you for attaining something that does. But love... Love doesn't assure your survival. Love even makes you turn your back on yourself. It is an entirely social concept. You cannot love something on your own. Love is something you *give*, love is something felt for something else. And what does it accomplish? The fuzzy feeling inside our tummies? The sense of peace and fulfillment? Why did we need to develop a concept such as love from a purely scientific point of view?

. . .

BUT THAT'S the beauty of it. We don't know. Yet this simple but profound concept is at the very core of all our lives. We don't know why, but we don't *need* to know why either. We are all perfectly happy just knowing what it feels like to love. Because love is such a wonderful thing to experience, even if it drives us to throw our logic to the wind and abandon all self-preservation instincts every other feeling of ours tries to keep. We all know it, we all have felt it, and we all spend our entire lives searching for it.

End of Sneak Peek.

Click Here to Continue Reading How to Love Yourself and Fall in Love NOW!

https://books2read.com/u/38yQP6